Just One Girl

MeiLee Martin

BookLeaf Publishing

Presentation by *BookLeaf Publishing*

Web: www.bookleafpub.com

E-mail: info@bookleafpub.com

ISBN: 9789395756440

First edition 2022

DEDICATION

This creation is dedicated to my mother, Dora, without whom I would be nothing. She has been my rock, and I am eternally grateful for all her love and support. I love you, Momma, and appreciate you more than I will ever be able to express.

ACKNOWLEDGEMENT

I want to thank my friends and family for supporting me throughout my writing journey. I want to give a special thanks to my husband, Joshua, for pushing me to do things I never thought I could do. Thank you, my love, for everything you do.

One Girl

I am only one girl
> a woman

I am only one heart
> one soul
>
> one mind

I have only one love
> that craves devotion

I am only one being
> searching
>
> hoping
>
> yearning for the same

Hummingbird

2

The hummingbird
Quick as a heartbeat
Quiet and timid, thoughtful
Just like her smile

Wren

The wren
Inquisitive and bold
Her opinions heard
Bravery and elegance combined.

Cardinal

The cardinal
Brilliant as the flame
That burned within her
Bold and brash against the monotonous snow
Bright and as loud as her laugh

House of Ghosts

This is a house of ghosts.
Memories, both bright and dark
    play like theatre in our minds.
Lives lived over and over again
    within these walls.
Trails of memories,
    walking the same halls I tread every day.
Choices defined by these imprinted walls
    and opinions long past.
This is my house, this house of ghosts.

My Mother's Quilt

Once beautifully and skillfully crafted,
Patience and time, purposefully taken.
Now worn and faded
Where once vibrant, comforts still.

Shelter and safety underneath,
Protection from untouchable things.
A light in the darkness of my mind
Borrowed and never returned,
Unmentioned, it's meaning just always
understood.

I lie beneath it on the dark days.
Nothing fixed, in reality
But feeling comfort all the same.
Restful, peaceful, safe, whole, at home.
Less torn or frayed like the edges of the
Quilt that covers me.

My Ghosts

My ghosts
Quiet, kind
Watchful, loving
The ones who left me alone here.

Loved, missed, never forgotten
Felt when the moment is right.
A scent caught and breath taken on
a bad day.

Their constant overcast,
Superimposed mist over my reality.
Memories imprinted on the foundation
    of my life.

My ghosts
Fading memories
But never lost to time
The ones who never leave me alone.

Half Lived

Half lived life
Lost little moments
Missed snatches of time
Partial thoughts that flit away
Forgotten words on the tip of your tongue

Stages

Intuition,
gut feelings,
something isn't right
Shock,
for a moment,
truth is revealed
Vindication,
confirmation,
knowing what was unknown
Devastation,
a whole future planned,
thrown away
Anger,
a life devoted and given,
taken for granted
Bitterness,
time wasted,
will never get back
Embarrassment,
Social disappointment,
What will they think?
Confusion
Was it not enough?
Could changes have been made?

Disgust,
selfish actions,
disregard for pain inflicted
Grief,
death of promises made,
a family broken
Guilt,
innocent hearts in pain,
I couldn't protect them
Acceptance,
I have all I need,
I am enough.
Relief,
living my full truth,
future full of potential.

Speak Your Mind

Speak your mind
Clarify, specify
Open up, breathe in deep
Let the thoughts out, take the leap.

Don't conceal how you feel
Communicate, annunciate
Make sure they know your
meaning.

Secrets break, while building walls
Don't bottle up, withhold
Keeping quiet only hurts
Instead, choose to be bold.

Unknown

Fear and the unknown are all I've ever known
The struggle, the fight to stay alive.
Others taking, breaking,
Taking all I'm giving.

Requiring ever more from me,
With little left over for me to thrive.

Broken trust and broken promises
Building walls too high to scale
Dreams shattered, broken,
Shattered time and time again.

Learning, at last, that I'm my only hero
Only I can push myself past the darkness
and prevail.

Four Letter Word

Love is a four letter word
When spoken from the wrong Lips

Lips that taste like sugar
But slowly spread their Poison

Poison that corrupts the heart
And bleeds into the Soul

A Soul that only craved
Someone to Love

Complete

My dark thoughts
Their bright smiles beam
All those broken promises
But all my bigger dreams
Pain of a shattered heart
But knowing, now, my soul's complete
Sometimes we fear the worst,
But we must always reject defeat.

My Last Baby

She walks away from me,
My last baby
Off on her first big adventure
Alone
Brave and beautiful
Wrapped in such a small package
Tiny fingers and toes once tickled
Now wear dance shoes to recitals
Cries letting me know I was needed
Replaced by laughter
Fading in the distance
First shaky steps, tiny hands holding my fingers
Now long and slender legs
Running, never looking back
Overwhelming pride, sadness
Remembering my last baby
All the years watching her learn and grow
Encouraging her thirst for knowledge,
Seeing her excitement and nerves
As she takes new steps away from me
Knowing she will do remarkable things.

Waiting

All the mom's in the car rider line
Waiting on our babies
This one is reading,
Thinking of dinner ideas
This one is scrolling,
Not thinking at all
One mom on the phone
Arguing with a husband who is secretly cheating
That mom is chain smoking
Dreading the abuse to come
This dad is waiting,
Thinking of the career given up for his wife's
One mom broke line, rushing
Just like she does through life
All of us waiting,
Loving the little faces that will light up when
they see us

Picture Perfect

The picture perfect life
Until the picture changes
The lies of a happy snapshot
Hiding the broken image beneath
A beautiful family album
With torn and tattered pages
Hidden truth can create monsters
With sharp and deadly teeth

Alone

I walk alone
I live alone among many
I am alone among all the chaos around me
I breathe alone
I dream alone
Amongst my loved ones, I am alone
Alone I read
I work alone
I take my time to think, alone
Loving those who love me,
I am still alone

Second Chance

My second chance
Heart break turned into broken walls
and open hearts
Blind, painful infatuation replaced by
soul filling, accepting love
Who I thought I was supposed to be
hidden and afraid
My true self, finally found and awakened
in new arms

Oblivion

I wake from oblivion
Finding scattered pieces of me
Torn over time
Stitched together
By unknown circumstances

There are remnants,
The many versions of me
That used to be
Glittered across this patchwork presence
In front of me

From oblivion I travel
Through madness to find what is missing,
Myself, lost to time, to pain, to others
Given away piece by precious piece
Asking for acceptance, rarely given

I have been broken
On the inside
Glued together
By the patience of those
That love me

Love me for me
Hidden by the blindness of ignorance
The pursuit of falsities
My hidden figures, patiently waiting
For me to awaken

Spice

When you look at me
I taste spices unknown to me
Love and lust rolled into one
Looking at me with eyes filled with emotions
Knowing that one spicy look says it all

Water

The tub fills slowly with cleansing water
Cascading healing, from the faucet,
Flowing over me
Ripples, bubbles kissing my toes,
Caressing my skin
Touches that make me feel whole again
Time and patience allow the water to release me
From tensions grasp
Piscean energy recharging
Refortifying me with the power to pursue
another day